The Welshpool & Llanfair Light Railway

Abortive Schemes, 1845-1887

Rail transport first reached Welshpool in 1817 – the short Welsh Pool Rail Road which
the town and for over thirty years carried granite from the Standard Quarry to the]
1840s, a frenzy of railway mania gripped the country with proposals for much grander
were proposed to bring rail communication to mid-Wales. In 1845, Isambard Kingdon. ᵤ. ᵤₙₑᵤ ᵤᵣₑw up plans for an
impressive scheme to lay broad gauge metals across the Welsh massif traversing the Banwy valley. The prize was Porth
Dinllaen, to be a new port for Ireland. Withdrawal of the parliamentary Bill deprived Llanfair Caereinion of early
possession of good communication with both the English lowlands and the Welsh coast. The little township on the bank
of the River Banwy deep in upland Powys served a far flung farming community, meanwhile retaining close ties with
the border market town of Welshpool, nine miles to the east across difficult terrain.

Welshpool was connected with the national network on 4 August 1860 with the opening of the Oswestry, Welchpool
and Newtown Railway, the LNWR also arriving from Shrewsbury in 1862. Within the next few years, a great deal of
agitation arose for rail links for many small towns and villages in the vicinity and the busy market centre of Llanfair
Caereinion (population 2,584) was no exception.

Within two years, local worthies led by Welshpool's mayor, were proposing a route from the new Welshpool station,
partly in tunnel under the town and climbing through the Pass of Golfa to reach the Banwy valley. At the instigation of
the Earl of Powis, the planned route was changed to run southwards from Welshpool station, skirting the south-eastern
flanks of the Powis estate before climbing the slopes of the Dysserth woods to Castle Caereinion. David Davies, the
renowned Welsh railway contractor, at first derided this scheme. Then, upon hearing of the success of the 1ft 11in gauge
Festiniog Railway with its newly introduced steam locomotives, he suggested narrow gauge as the best way to make a
railway to Llanfair. The amended plan would have involved a section of mixed gauge track to give trains access to
Welshpool station. The Bill was deposited for parliamentary scrutiny in 1864 but was doomed by insufficient financial
support and opposition from those who wanted a standard gauge line reaching Llanfair from the north.

A decade later, another attempt made better progress, receiving an Act to authorise construction on 10 August 1877.
Based on the Dysserth woods route, it was to be a 'light' railway, maximum speed 20mph, 9.6 miles long from Llanfair
to the junction with the Cambrian Railways a mile south of Welshpool. Alas, finances flagged and even an attempt to
convert to a narrow gauge version was of no avail.

But ten years on, yet another scheme for this route with narrow gauge metals, was promoted by a firm of London civil
engineers. Its Act received royal approval on 23 August 1887 but was no more successful than previous schemes in
attracting financial backing.

Birth Pangs, 1896-1903

The turning-point was the passing of the Light Railways Act on 14 August 1896. Its aim was to foster the construction
of simple lines of railway to develop penurious areas, using public subsidy – a progenitor, perhaps, of modern day
European regional policy. Imposing low speed limits allowed onerous railway regulations to be waived in the interests
of economy. Land had to be acquired without charge as far as possible and an existing company had to build and
operate each line.

Two rival schemes quickly emerged for railways to Llanfair Caereinion. The first, backed by the inhabitants of
Llanfair, was the standard gauge Llanfair and Meifod Light Railway proposal, based on a route with less difficult grades

from the Cambrian's main line at Arddleen north of Welshpool and using the Vyrnwy and Banwy valleys to reach Llanfair. Meanwhile, meetings in Welshpool supported a Welshpool and Llanfair Light Railway scheme using the most direct route, by the roadside, continental style. Much shorter and with steep gradients to negotiate, from the outset they planned it to be 2ft 6in gauge but with transporter wagons (never actually acquired) to minimise the disadvantage of the break of gauge. This rivalry meant a public inquiry by the Light Railway Commissioners. Held in the Board School at Llanfair Caereinion, it was twelve months later, on 4 September 1897, that the decision was announced in favour of the Welshpool scheme. And not until the autumn of 1899 was the Light Railway Order confirmed after details of the provisions in the Order had been worked out and negotiations concluded for the Cambrian Railways Company to work the line. Grants and loans had also to be negotiated with the Treasury (eventually covering 40% of the cost of construction) and loans and share issues arranged with local authorities in the area (34%) with ordinary shareholders and debenture holders accounting for the smaller portion remaining.

Construction took nearly two years but the Board of Trade's Major Druitt was not satisfied on his first inspection in February 1903. Even on a return visit later that month he asked for modifications to check rails on sharp curves but on 9 March, a small crowd cheered the departure of *The Countess* with the first freight train from Welshpool, loaded with grain and coal.

Common Carrier for a Rural Community, 1903-56

On 3 April 1903, the Board of Trade certified the line fit for public traffic. It was just over 9 miles long, rising 360 ft in the relentless three mile climb out of Welshpool. Economies permitted under the Light Railways legislation – not to mention the frustrating shortfall in funds raised – resulted in the W&LLR coming to have a character and a charm of a quite individual nature. All roads were crossed on the level and even gates were dispensed with in most places. Signalling, too, was a luxury that could not be afforded – the line was worked with a wooden staff and a one-engine-in-steam system. Speed limits were restrictive – 20mph under the Order and though later increased it was reduced to 15 mph in the last decade or so of freight operation. Lower limits locally marked the twisting and turning of the line as it exploited the flexibility of the narrow gauge to overcome physical obstacles. Gravelled 'landing places' served for platforms and corrugated iron cubicles did duty as station buildings.

Operation of the line was in the hands of the Cambrian Railways Co. until the end of 1922. At first, four mixed trains ran each way on weekdays – never on Sundays. However, finances faltered and passenger services were reduced as early as 1909 and again towards the end of World War I. With the passing of the Grouping of Railways Act in 1921, the Cambrian – and the nominally still independent W&LLR Co. – were to be absorbed by the Great Western Railway. The W&LLR Co. received £23,236 for the transfer of ownership allowing less than full repayment of loans outstanding for twenty years - and barely 25p in the pound to shareholders.

Not too pleased with such an unpromising acquisition, the GWR began experimenting with a bus service in 1925 and initiated a review of the line's future. A thrice weekly evening train introduced in 1920, was cut first. Hard on its heels came the announcement in 1931 that all passenger services were to be axed from 7th February. It caused an outcry locally. Though this proved futile, at least the railway had escaped complete closure. So, for twenty-five years, the line lived on as a freight only branch with one movement of its increasingly decrepit wagons each way on most days. Its fate was reconsidered several times but it was left to BR, after nationalisation in 1948, to decide that, at last, the end should come. Others, fortunately, had different ideas.

2. Welshpool's Main Line Station, 1974

Opened in 1860 by the Oswestry, Welchpool & Newtown Railway, this imposing edifice was to be the interchange for the W&LLR's passengers. The freight yards and the narrow gauge line, were to the left of the picture. The building later served the Cambrian Railways, the L&NWR, the GWR – and British Rail until 1992.

3. The Beginning

Great celebrations accompanied the cutting of the first sod near the Welshpool terminus on 30 May 1901. Not only railway officials were present but MPs, councillors, landowners, magistrates, the fire brigade *et al*. The young Viscount Clive, with his parents the Earl and Countess of Powis nearby, is helped to perform the ceremony while the band of the Montgomeryshire Imperial Yeomanry plays. [Courtesy: Peter Coward]

4. Building the Underbridges, c.1901

The construction contract had been awarded to John Strachan of Cardiff. About a hundred men were engaged and within two months work was advancing on the bridges and smaller structures. Soon after this cattle creep on Golfa bank was completed, temporary rails were laid from Welshpool along the section.
[W&LLR Pres. Co.]

5. Construction Nears the Summit

A brief rest for the navvies working on the shallow cutting between Golfa and Sylfaen. The gangs worked 10 hours a day for 5s 10d (29p). Relaxation could be boisterous: in 1902, their off duty drinking and revelling caused local villagers to enlist the help of the police for protection.

6. First Rails, c.1902

At several locations simultaneously, temporary track was worked by horses until the formation was sufficiently advanced for Strachan's little locomotives to be employed. To minimise costs, cuttings were made only when unavoidable and embankments were low. Wet weather caused slips which delayed completion.

7. The Welshpool Shunter

Strachan No. 3 was a standard gauge Hunslet 0-4-0 saddle tank built in 1885. Used at Welshpool during the building of the W&LLR, it presumably worked on the delivery sidings from the main line. It seems to have moved afterwards to the Tanat Valley Light Railway to the north.
[W&LLR Pres. Co.]

8. Building the River Bridge, 1902
The girder viaduct over the wayward River Banwy was completed in 1902 after the Cambrian Railways insisted on the piers being rebuilt in view of the 'perishable nature' of the stone first used. The device on the left raised water for Strachan's engines. *Strachan No. 8*, builder unknown, stands on the right hand side of the bridge.

9. Handling the Construction Trains

In September 1901, contractor Strachan took delivery of 2ft 6in gauge 0-4-0ST *Strachan No. 9* from W. G. Bagnall Ltd. It worked on the construction project and did not leave until after the opening of the line. In due course, it moved to Jees Granite & Brick Co Ltd near Nuneaton, becoming *Butcher* (as photographed) and putting in a thirty year stint before its demise. Strachan also operated a narrow gauge four coupled Hunslet saddle tank on the project.
[Collection: Frank Jones]

10. The Canal Bridge, 1970
This steel girder plate bridge, span 33ft 4in, was built across the Montgomeryshire Canal after the Cambrian Railways Co. vetoed plans for a swing bridge. They agreed to a siding to the canalside which was never built.

11. Getting Through the Town
With a longitudinal bridge covering the Lledan Brook, the track squeezed between the cottages; but when trains ran, washing was in danger of being smothered in smuts and had to be retrieved hurriedly from back yards.
[John Clemmens]

12. Getting Through the Town

Welshpool's Church Street (middle distance) lost a house, demolished to provide a route for the new railway. By straddling the Lledan Brook further demolition was avoided. The structure of the bridge was exposed when a road was made here in modern times.
[G. S. Chadwick]

13. Welshpool Map

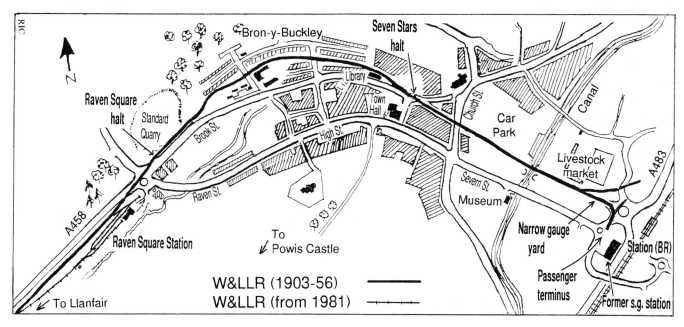

RIC

N

Bron-y-Buckley

Seven Stars halt

Library

Raven Square halt

Standard Quarry

Town Hall

Brook St.

High St.

Church St.

Car Park

Canal

Livestock market

A483

Severn St.

Museum

A458

Raven Square Station

Raven St.

To Powis Castle

Narrow gauge yard

Passenger terminus

Station (BR)

Former s.g. station

To Llanfair

W&LLR (1903-56) ⎯⎯⎯⎯

W&LLR (from 1981) ⟊⟊⟊⟊⟊

14. Golfa Incline, c.1903
A mile of 1 in 29 (the steepest section of the Cambrian Railways system) carried the line past the Black Pools, once a reservoir for Welshpool. Sharp reverse curves made the climb even more difficult. The Powis woods are in the background.

15. Map of the line

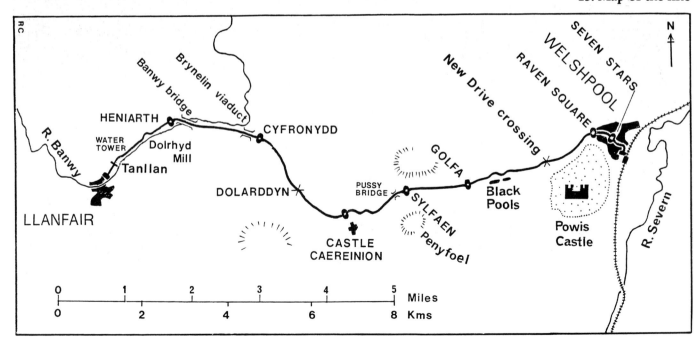

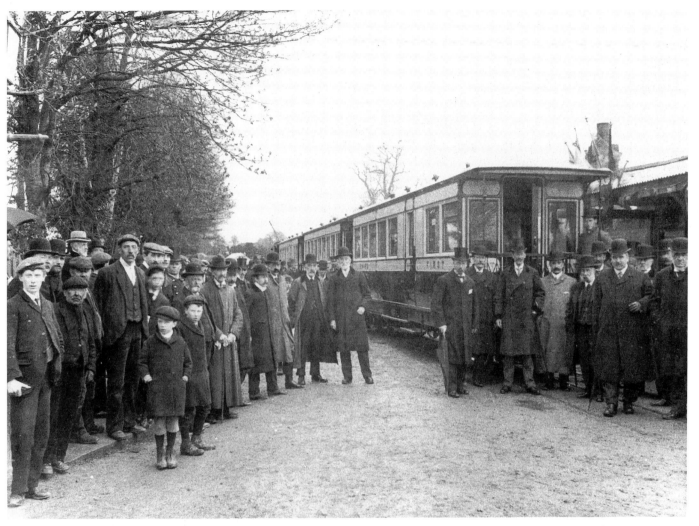

16. The Opening Ceremony

The great day was 4th April 1903 and there were tremendous celebrations. The Earl of Powis, W&LLR directors and representatives of the Cambrian Railways Co. (to the right) were present, contrasting with more lowly townspeople. The train started in Smithfield Road – the W&LLR was too poor to provide a proper station. There was a gravel platform and (for ten years) a waiting room-cum-booking office.

[Powysland Museum]

17. Welshpool's Narrow Gauge Goods Yard, 1952

The curve to the right led to the passenger terminus and was still in situ when this picture was taken. Off the picture to the left, the Monday livestock market was served by the standard gauge siding which ran across Smithfield Road in the background into the main line goods yard. For many years after 1908, it was mixed gauge so that W&LLR trains could reach Boys and Boden's sawmills beside the main line – and the cattle transfer dock. Behind the locomotive, is the water column and loco shed. One of the line's two brake vans stands on the stub which once gave access to the carriage shed behind. [Maurice Deane]

18. Llanfair Station c.1903
Soon after the line opened, a rake of private owner wagons stands on the siding leading to the goods shed (in its original shorter form). The simple ramp for loading cattle was later replaced by a larger stone-faced dock. For passengers, only a low level platform is provided.
[W&LLR Pres. Co.]

19. Passenger Facilities, c.1903
The utilitarian corrugated iron booking office at Llanfair.

20. Locomotives –
The Countess, **1902**
Before the preservation era, the original locomotives, built in 1902, were the only ones to work the line. Although the Cambrian Railways asked for three, the W&LLR could only afford the two which Beyer Peacock & Co supplied for £1,630 each. No. 2 *The Countess* was photographed at the makers' Gorton Works, Manchester, before being finished in the Cambrian Railways' livery of black, lined chrome yellow. The Walschaerts valve gear was new to the British narrow gauge scene. [W&LLR Pres. Co.]

21. Locomotives – *The Earl*
The locomotives were identical even after rebuilding at Swindon Works in 1929/30. No.1 *The Earl* became GWR No. 822 as seen here. The GWR fitted a new boiler, with increased heating surface, a copper-capped parallel chimney, a large steam dome and safety valves enclosed in a brass 'trumpet'.
[Real Photographs/Ian Allan]

22. The Loco Shed, 1956

Built of corrugated iron, the only shed, at Welshpool, was just big enough to house the two locomotives. Some maintenance work was done here (more so in later years); though there were inspection pits, there was little else in the way of workshop facilities. A primitive heater for the water column can be seen.
[W&LLR Pres. Co./Keith Catchpole]

23. Early Days: Passenger Service, 1909

The Countess with the third class coach and one of the composites at the first water tower close to Dolrhyd Mill. On Mondays (Welshpool's market day), trains were well patronised – often packed with passengers clutching baskets of cheese, butter, and eggs and hampers of chickens. The Cambrian Railways Co. asked for a fourth coach to be provided but there was no money for this.
[S. P. Higgins Collection/National Railway Museum, York]

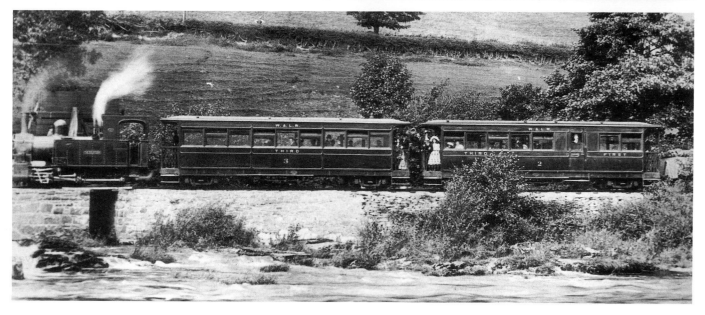

24. Cambrian Days, Llanfair Station

Soon after opening, this scene at Llanfair Caereinion shows how passengers were usually catered for with mixed trains, an economical arrangement. Here, the train is headed by *The Earl*. But for the first ten years at least, the Cambrian Railways Co. operated the line at a loss while the W&LLR share-holders never received a dividend.
[Real Photographs/ Ian Allan]

25. Cambrian Days, Timber Traffic, c.1909

The carriage of round timber by passenger or mixed trains was forbidden. Timber trains were not to exceed 10mph: lengths greater than two wagons needed a match truck and if longer than three wagons, two separated trucks connected by a drag chain were employed. Loading took place at Tanllan, just east of Llanfair, at Heniarth and occasionally elsewhere. Presumably, *The Earl*, seen in Welshpool yard c.1909, has run round the train prior to shunting to the stacking grounds across Smithfield Road.
[Real Photographs/ Ian Allan]

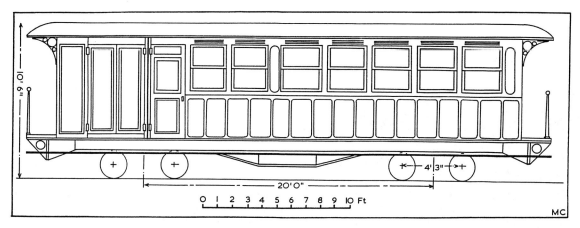

26. Coaching Stock: Plans, 1901

The first plans for the composite coach included a section for luggage at the expense of having less third

27. Coaching Stock: In Service

Three quite splendid bogie coaches were built for the line by R.Y. Pickering & Co. of Lanarkshire.
Built on steel frames, the saloon bodies were constructed of oak and mahogany, 30ft long.
One of the two composite coaches is seen in post-1909 Cambrian Railways livery. Its third class seats were
lathed with backs to the windows but the first class had simple upholstery.
The small size of the guard's compartment between the first and third saloons meant that the
goods brake van was often needed for 'smalls' traffic. Coach No. 3 was third class only with 46 seats.

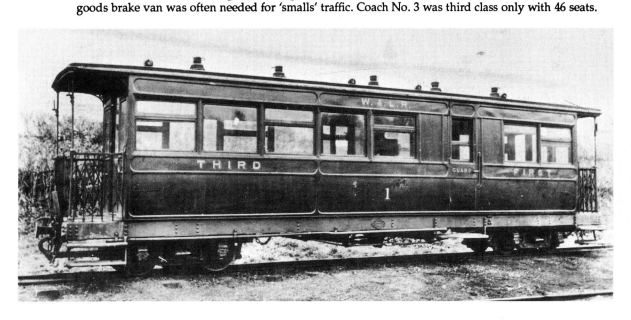

Welshpool & Llanfair Light Railway (Narrow Gauge.)

Miles from Welshpool		DOWN.		1 Goods A	3 Goods 1st & 3rd Mons. in month.	5 ¶ Mixed	7 Mixed Mons. except.	9 Mixed Mons. only.	11 Mixed	13 Mixed
M.	C.			a.m.	a.m.	a.m.	a.m.	p.m.	p.m.	p.m.
		Welshp'l Station dep	..	5 10	6 0	8 10	11 45	12 45	3 55	7 5
	35	Welshp'l Sev' St's ,,	..	..	...	*	*	*	*	*
1	0	Raven Square .. ,,	..	..	...	*	*	*	*	*
1	66	Golfa .. .. ,,	..	..	...	*	*	*	*	*
3	59	Sylfaen Halt .. ,,	..	.	...	*	*	*	*	*
4	65	Castle Caereinion ,,	..	..	...	8 30	12 5	1 5	4 15	7 25
6	57	Cyfronydd .. ,,	..	..	...	*	*	*	*	*
7	54	Heniarth.. .. ,,	..	..	...	*	*	*	*	*
9	4	Llanfair .. .. ar	..	6 15	7 10	9 5	12 40	1 40	4 50	7 55

Miles from Llanfair.		UP.		2 Mixed. A	4 Mixed 1st & 3-d Mons. in month.	6 Mixed	8 Mixed	10 Mixed	12 Goods. Thurs. & Sats. excepted.	14 Mixed Thurs. & Sats. & Llanfair Fair Days.
M.	C.			a.m.	a.m.	a.m.	p.m.	p.m.	p.m.	p.m.
		Llanfair .. ..dep	..	6 30	7 30	9 40	2 15	5 30	8 10	8 0
1	10	Heniarth .. ,,	..	*	*	*	*	*	..	*
2	27	Cyfronydd . ,,	..	*	*	*	*	*	..	*
4	20	Castle Caereinion ,,	..	6 50	7 50	10 0	2 35	5 50	..	8 25
5	26	Sylfaen Halt .. ,,	..	*	*	*	*	*	..	*
6	19	Golfa .. .. ,,	..	*	*	*	*	*	..	*
8	5	Raven Square .. ,,	..	*	*	*	*	*	..	*
8	50	Welshp'l Sev' St's ,,	..	*	*	*	*	*	..	*
9	4	Welshpool Station arr	..	7 20	8 20	10 30	3 5	6 20	9 25	8 55

* Trains **must stop** at all stations to pick up or set down passengers.

¶ On Llanfair Fair days No. 5 will run 20 minutes earlier, and on First and Third Mondays in each month 25 minutes later.

A—Runs on Fourth Monday in November, February, and May only.

On Mondays all Up and Down trains will stop at the Crossing at Dolarddyn to pick up or set down passengers to or from Welshpool. Passengers must take Cyfronydd tickets. Trains will also stop at Dolarddyn on other days for picnic parties.   S.88701.

28. Timetable, 1915

The Cambrian Railways working timetable as it appeared in October 1915 showing how the line was worked with one engine in steam only. For many years, the basic pattern consisted of four trains each way on weekdays. At times, the additional very early departure from Welshpool ran as a Mixed train. In 1917, trains nos. 12, 13 and 14 were removed from the timetable.
[S.P.Higgins Collection/National Railway Museum,York]

29. In Welshpool

Emerging from 'The Narrows' where the line was built over the Lledan Brook, this train, early in the Cambrian era, is crossing Union Street to reach Seven Stars, the first halt, going westwards.

On the Llanfair Railway, Welshpool

30. No Trains Today!

Seven Stars Halt, the 'town station' took its name from the public house demolished to make way for the railway. Floods, possibly in 1919, have covered the track. A corner of a shelter of some sort is visible on the right.

WELSHPOOL SEVEN STARS

BOVRIL

31. Seven Stars Survivor, 1971
The waiting shelter at Seven Stars was converted for other use after the end of passenger services. Passengers had little protection until about 1912.

32. The Open Wagons, 1902
In contrast to the passenger stock, the freight vehicles were all rather rudimentary, based on a 4-wheeled, timber framed design. Builders R. Y. Pickering & Co. advised against the wooden block buffers originally specified. Side chains were an afterthought and the springs were only added after delivery. The curved strapping on the wagons disappeared when the GWR rebuilt the wagons. Forty 4-ton wagons were supplied, some later subjected to adaptation.
[R. Y. Pickering & Co. Ltd.]

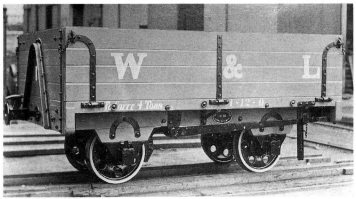

33. Private Owner Wagons, 1903
Private owner wagons were rare on British narrow gauge lines but soon after opening, Pickerings supplied five wagons for a local coal merchant.
[R. Y. Pickering & Co. Ltd]

34. Timber Transport, c.1930

Six timber bolster wagons arrived in April 1904 but the W&LLR could not afford the remainder of the ten ordered. Instead they are believed to have cut down four of the openbwagons. In 1924, the GWR built six more, this time with steel frames.
[Real Photographs/Ian Allan]

35. Cattle Vans, 1902

Two timber built covered vans were supplied in 1902, each intended for the carriage of seven cattle. This was a pessimistic forecast of how many would be needed. Six open wagons were adapted for cattle in 1930 while two covered vans with steel underframes and body framing were added to the fleet by the GWR after first being allocated to the Vale of Rheidol Railway.
[R. Y. Pickering & Co Ltd]

36. Livestock Wagon, 1949

The Cambrian Railways Co. converted eight open wagons for carrying sheep, the first batch in 1911. The slatted sides and ends were removable and a fully planked door (on the other side in the picture) dropped down to form a ramp.
[S. P. Higgins Collection/ National Railway Museum, York]

37. The Brake Vans, 1902
The makers' photograph shows one of
the line's two brake vans as built with an
open balcony; a central sliding door was
quickly added but some time during the
Cambrian era the van body was
extended to cover the balcony
and the sliding doors were resited.
[R. Y. Pickering & Co. Ltd.]

38. Goods Vans, 1902
The four closed vans, also from
Lanarkshire, were constructed in oak,
clad with white pine, and provided
with a sliding door.
[R. Y. Pickering & Co. Ltd.]

39. Welshpool Terminus, c.1925
GWR No. 823 *Countess* (its name now abbreviated) heads the waiting train: in GWR days, mixed trains continued to be the normal formation. In 1913, the passenger terminus had been moved out of Smithfield Road into the Cambrian Railways goods yard.
[Real Photographs/Ian Allan]

40. Westward Ho!
Welshpool Yard, c.1930
GWR No. 822 *The Earl* passes through the narrow gauge goods yard to begin the 1 in 33 climb to the canal bridge. Standard gauge cattle wagons stand on the mixed gauge Smithfield siding behind.
[Real Photographs/Ian Allan]

41. Leaving the Town

Raven Square halt was in Brook Street near the Standard Quarry. This 1920s view shows GWR No. 823 *Countess* unusually working bunker first towards Llanfair. In 1926, the GWR took a hard look at the line's future, reduced all work to one 8 hour shift per day and eventually announced that after 7th February 1931, no more passenger trains would run.

42. Empties to Welshpool, 1952

Freight trains usually ran at least once a day after 1931: except for timber and livestock trains, empty stock predominated in eastward workings. Running across Smithfield Road into the standard gauge yard gave access to the transship sidings.
[Maurice Dean]

43. The Transship Shed, c.1950
This was on the eastern side of a triangle which could be temporarily completed using a moveable section of rail. Coaches were said to have been turned round it to equalise wheel wear.

44. Manhandling
Coal was the predominant freight traffic westbound. At Welshpool, Dick Stephens transfers a load for Llanfair the hard way.
[Ireta Richards/Don Griffiths]

45. Welshpool Goods Shed, c.1952

The narrow gauge yard at Welshpool was provided with the corrugated iron warehouse beside these cattle vans. Access for road vehicles was on the other side, reached from Smithfield Road. [Maurice Dean]

46. Dual Purpose Formation, 1971

The mixed gauge Smithfield siding crossed the road making the north side of 'the triangle'. The derelict cattle transfer dock is on the left.

47. Livestock Traffic, 1947

In GWR days, some 200 wagons of sheep and lambs, not to mention loads of cattle, were moved annually. The traffic peaked during the petrol-starved days of World War II but was tailing off when No. 822 *The Earl* was photographed climbing Sylfaen bank in 1947. The train includes vehicles converted from open wagons, two of which have been strengthened for cattle.
[S. P. Higgins Collection/ National Railway Museum, York]

48. Near the Standard Quarry, 1954

In 1948, the line became part of the newly created British Railways. Trains continued to run daily surprising the steadily growing stream of motorists at Welshpool's road crossings. Here, wagons of coal and bricks and vans loaded with agricultural supplies are approaching the quarry in Brook Street. Until it closed c.1930, roadstone was collected from here and there was a siding for the purpose. Raven Square lies ahead.
[W&LLR Pres. Co.]

49. Llanfair Yard c.1950
In the yard at Llanfair, *Countess* has a respite while fireman Fred Williams and guard R. Morgan confer with local merchant M. L. Peate. Some of the wagons have been shunted under the three part canopy for unloading into the warehouse. Further storage for grain and feedstuffs was provided in the 1940s in the condemned standard gauge coach bodies grounded on the right.
[By permission of the National Library of Wales/Trwy ganiatad Llyfrgell Genediaethol Cymru]

50. Castle Caereinion, c.1952

Idyllic scene: *Countess* simmering gently while some new gates are unloaded. The corrugated iron shelter is a reminder of pre-1931 passenger services and the distant signal box is a relic of a 1907 scheme for passing trains here, aborted for reasons of economy. Behind No. 823 is the cattle loading ramp: and the loop where wagons of coal and slag (for fertiliser) were left for unloading. The line's steep gradients and sharp curves limited trains to a maximum of seven wagons of coal and minerals or eleven wagons and vans of general merchandise. [Maurice Dean]

51. Accommodation for Farmers
Near Castle Caereinion, the line's only overbridge linked divided landholdings. It imposed a maximum loading height of 12ft. It was demolished in 1932.

52. Passengers No More, c.1950
Though continuing to serve the freight traffic, Llanfair yard wears a melancholy air. The former waiting room on the left became a store. Beyond it, a plank links the van to a galvanised iron shed into which sacks of meal and grain will be unloaded.

53. Human Resources, c.1950
Most of the line's staff were included in this pre-closure photograph at Llanfair – the locomotive crew, guard, platelayers and the 'Railman i/c Llanfair station.'
[W&LLR Pres. Co./N.Evans]

54. Mechanical Assistance, 1956
In the freight-only era, one gang maintained the whole line replacing one or two sleepers at a time, repairing the fences and mowing the grass. In 1940, they were provided with this Wickham trolley with 350cc JAP petrol engine under the seat. Here, in March 1956, it was running as BR No. 109W.
[Hugh Ballantyne]

55. Rail to Road, 1956

At Llanfair in April 1956, agricultural supplies are collected by a local merchant. With closure looming, the goods van on the coal wharf is clearly worse for wear. Traffic now consisted of only three or four trains each week.
[J.E.Tennent]

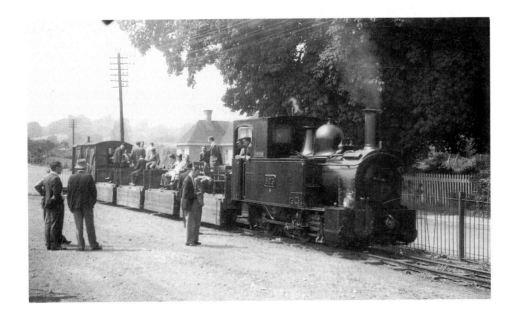

56. Excursions

Countess waits at Welshpool on 2nd July 1949 for a party of Birmingham Locomotive Club members arriving on an ex-GWR diesel railcar. Seats from Welshpool main line station were placed back to back in the open wagons to accommodate them. The first of several, such excursions in freight wagons would never have been countenanced today!
[W&LLR Pres. Co./S. H. Keyse]

57. Homeward Bound – Raven Square, c.1954

During the years after nationalisation, the need for costly locomotive repairs and competition from motor transport brought nearer the prospect of closure. Rumours of such a move attracted enthusiasts to the line. After descending the notorious Golfa incline (in unfitted stock!) this special crosses Raven Square roundabout where later the line was to be cut.
[Ivo Peters]

58. Last Rites, 1956

The farewell trip was assigned to the Stephenson Locomotive Society on 3rd November 1956. The Newtown Silver Band played at Welshpool and intermediate points and 120 society members filled the nine little wagons and two brakevans. On the way back, *The Earl* paused at the water tower near Llanfair and eventually returned to Welshpool, whistling all the way through the town to the terminus where the main line engines joined in and the band finished the day with Handel's Funeral March. Never was there such a big finale for such a little railway!
[Ivo Peters]

59. Hibernation, 1959
Countess was removed to the former Cambrian Railways Oswestry Works early in 1956 when closure seemed likely but *The Earl* remained at Welshpool for a while. In 1958, the two locomotives were reunited. It was indeed fortunate that, instead of being cut up, they were stored here in safety awaiting a new future.
[G.W.Morrison]

60. Quarter Mile Posts
Distances were shown from Welshpool (Smithfield Road)
– miles above and quarters below.
'Milepost' 7¹/₄ is GWR pattern.
[R.Cragg]

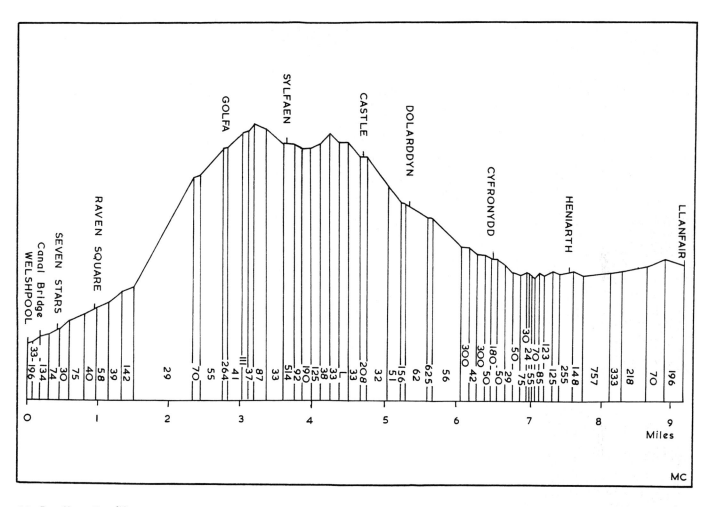

61. Gradient Profile

The line as completed. Surprisingly steep gradients were planned and in building, some became even steeper. At Welshpool, the terminus today is 150 yards east of the original Raven Square halt.

62. Using Horse Power, 1959
As the first working parties began clearing the line of undergrowth, some of the freight vehicles were saved from scrapping. But with neither motive power nor legal powers to operate, members of the Preservation Society borrowed a pair of sturdy cart horses which struggled through the town to move stock to Raven Square.
[C. J. Gammell]

63. Austin Trolley, 1961
The delays in getting started were frustrating but some volunteers decided to provide motive power by building this short-lived trolley. Completed in 1961, it had a 10hp petrol engine. The new company's first chairman, Lt. Col. Sir Thomas Salt, is on the left.
[Don Griffiths]

64. First Trains
No. 3 *Raven* arrived in March 1961 and was used to move the stock up the line as it was acquired. Here, some of the original 4-wheel wagons and an ex-Upnor & Lodge Hill bogie flat have reached Golfa. Eventually, the 16/20hp Ruston & Hornsby diesel became redundant and left in 1974.
[W&LLR Pres Co]

65. Members' Special, 1962
All the ex-Upnor stock was available for this crowded Special heading out of Welshpool across Raven Square on 31 March 1962 hauled by No. 1 *The Earl*. Another six months were to pass before sister locomotive *The Countess* returned.
[Hugh Ballantyne]

After 1956: Rescue and Evolution

The idea of trying to save the W&LLR first surfaced in the early 1950s although the only previous attempt to take over a doomed railway was that of the Talyllyn Railway Society. Furthermore, the W&LLR was different - it was state owned and 'privatisation' had not then been heard of. The endeavours of first the Narrow Gauge Railway Society and then the Branch Line Society fanned interest and as a result, some of the enthusiasts who rode in open wooden wagons on the special trips to Llanfair came together and formed a society to acquire the line just as it was closing. Pioneers that they were, they faced daunting legal and financial problems.

What's more, the track was in lamentable condition, no passenger carriages had survived and local authorities were opposed to the restoration of the line through Welshpool town. The stock actually available consisted of antiquated freight wagons and vans in Welshpool yard earmarked for scrapping. Searching elsewhere was difficult in view of the the gauge of 2ft 6ins, rare in Britain, and the line had no repair facilities to enable extensive rebuilding or regauging to be contemplated. However, by a timely coincidence, the Admiralty's Upnor and Lodge Hill Railway of the same gauge was closing and contacts existed which managed to secure the transfer of suitable vehicles.

Probing their way through such impediments, these dogged founder members came to realize that they needed to turn their simple organisation into a body with a more appropriate legal status so in 1960 the W&LLR Preservation Co Ltd was formed. This was a prerequisite to the Light Railway (Leasing and Transfer) Order which was eventually issued on 3 October 1962. The solution which had been achieved, six years after closure, was lease of the line west of Welshpool's Raven Square at lenient rates for 25 years. Elated, Company members offered a passenger service in December 1962 from Castle Caereinion to Llanfair for the Christmas fair. Efforts were then concentrated on preparing for the grand opening, four months later.

More sadly, a little later, on 17 August 1963, the last train of all ran through Welshpool's streets, spectacularly doubleheaded by the two Beyer Peacocks and lifting of the town section began almost immediately. Not originally regarded as the ideal headquarters for the project, Llanfair Caereinion station was gradually developed over many years. At first, visitors shared the minimal car parking space with merchants' coal heaps, there were no workshops or covered accommodation for the rolling stock and only basic passenger facilities. All this was to change.

Although the principle of all-volunteer operation was adopted, the enterprise faced many years of struggle and financial stringency. The company was undercapitalised and, being outside the main tourist areas, could only expect to achieve modest levels of traffic. However, the line's popularity grew steadily and without reserve funds for major repairs to locomotives Nos. 1 and 2, the search for more motive power and coaching stock spread far afield, early efforts bringing the Franco-Belge locomotive and the Zillertalbahn coaches to Wales. Successful acquisitions later from other countries included a complete train from Sierra Leone in 1975 as traffic reached a peak of 46,716 passengers carried in the year.

Meanwhile, a general appeal, support from public funds and a steadily increasing membership saw the line purchased from British Rail in 1973 while the granting of charity status in due course helped to husband resources.

Re-opening had proceeded in stages, despite almost being aborted following the bridge disaster of 1964. When regular passenger services began running all the way again between Llanfair and Welshpool, twenty five years had elapsed since closure by British Railways.

66. Members' Special, 1961

When the Admiralty's Lodge Hill & Upnor line closed, four semi-open coaches, a saloon coach, seven bogie wagons and two vans were obtained for the W&LLR. Some of this stock arrived (by rail) in July 1961 – together with No. 1 *The Earl* from Oswestry Works. This Special, pausing at the old Water Tower, on 23 September, was the first steam working since closure.

[W&LLR Pres Co]

67. Llanfair Station, c.1962

While re-opening was awaited, neglect had created a forlorn scene. On the right, the three decrepit standard gauge van and coach bodies, installed by the GWR, remain in situ. The coal heaps belonged to local merchants.

[R. Johnson]

68. (Facing) Public Trains Again, 1963

The re-opening ceremony was on 6 April. This special train (with No. 1 *The Earl*) in the old goods yard beside Welshpool Smithfield market was provided for the 5th Earl of Powis and guests and was one of the last passenger-carrying trains through the centre of Welshpool. Within a few months the town section was gone. [Maurice Deane]

69. In Welshpool, 1963

Over the brook and through 'the Narrows' (now demolished), the Re-opening Day train heads for Llanfair Caereinion where there were speeches and a ceremonial tape-cutting by the Earl of Powis. [John Clemmens]

70. Sylfaen Shunter

In 1964, there was a short-lived service to Sylfaen where tickets were sold from an original W&LLR brake van. With only a siding, No. 4 *Upnor Castle* helped with the turn round of trains. This 105 bhp diesel had arrived from the Lodge Hill & Upnor Railway in 1962 and also helped on works trains until sold to the Festiniog Railway in 1968. [W&LLR Pres Co]

71. Remedy for Disaster, 1965

After the first season, when trains ran successfully each weekend between Llanfair Caereinion and Castle Caereinion, services were extended to Sylfaen but, in December 1964, came a cruel reverse. Floods caused the near collapse of the Banwy river bridge. Only help with the rebuilding from the Army's Royal Engineers (16th Railway Regiment) prevented the whole project being abandoned. The completed construction can be seen in view no. 77.

[W&LLR Pres Co]

72. No. 7 *Chattenden*, 1985

The Drewry diesel proved invaluable for handling heavy engineering trains which were needed for the rebuilding of the track, following years of neglect. *Chattenden* also proved to be a vital stand-by for the passenger service. Built in 1949 for the Admiralty's Upnor line, it came from a military depot at Broughton Moor, Cumberland, in 1968, as a replacement for *Upnor Castle*. A newer engine, a 150bhp Gardner 6LXB, was fitted in 1980 and the cab was rebuilt with a rear entrance and steps.

73. At Heniarth, 1965

No. 1 *The Earl* returns from Castle Caereinion soon after the resumption of services over the river bridge on 14 August. During rebuilding, passenger services were restricted to the section between Llanfair and Heniarth, sometimes handled by the vertical boilered Sentinel *Nutty*, seen here on an engineering train.

[W&LLR Pres Co]

74. Another Diesel, 1971

No. 9 *Wynnstay* at Castle Caereinion: occasionally diesel haulage was necessary when a steam locomotive failed unexpectedly. This 1951 Fowler product, intended for service in East Africa, was diverted to a Glamorgan cement works before arriving at Llanfair in 1969. Proving less than ideal for work on the line, the locomotive moved elsewhere three years later.

75. Workshops, 1968

In 1967, a site was excavated in the slopes on the south east edge of Llanfair station for a locomotive shed and workshops. Second-hand steelwork was erected by volunteers: it took four years to complete the shed shown in the background in picture no. 76.
[W&LLR Pres Co]

76. Castle Caereinion, 1968
The Countess prepares to return to Llanfair: though some distance from the village the station used to serve, modern travellers appreciate its scenic delights. Good run-round facilities favoured its new role as the terminus in the era following the bridge disaster and maintenance and improvement work were concentrated on the Llanfair-Castle section.

77. Coaches from Austria, 1968
Contacts with the Zillertalbahn resulted in the gift of five coaches in all, four of which are seen being dispatched by rail. They arrived at Welshpool BR goods yard and were then moved by road, one by one, to New Drive crossing for transfer to the W&LLR. Coach B27 followed in 1975. Built 1900-06 (B24 in 1925), their charm and character quickly established their popularity.
[Zillertalbahn]

78. *Sîr Drefaldwyn*, 1990
Arriving in Wales in December 1969, the locomotive was built in 1944 in France as a tender-tank for the German Military Railways. It worked on the Austrian Salzkammergut and Steiermärkische lines. It continues to carry 699.01, its Austrian fleet number, but has been named, in Welsh, after its new homeland, Montgomeryshire. This 27 ton machine has a wheelbase of only 8ft 10ins which, together with a pivoted axle and two flangeless wheels, allows easy negotiation of sharp curves.

79. Austrian Train, 1975
On the Banwy river bridge, No. 10 *Sîr Drefaldwyn* heads eastward with some of the Austrian coaches. The lattice steel pier of the bridge contrasts with the surviving stone pier.

80. Sylfaen, 1972

The track east of Castle Caereinion had to be reconstructed before services were extended to Sylfaen on 15 July 1972. There was still only a siding here so a second locomotive was again employed to allow the train engine to move round. Hand shunting was an emergency procedure! The nearest coach was the ex-Upnor 'Combination car' built for the comfort of naval officers.

81. Sylfaen, 1992

In 1976, Sylfaen Halt was reconstructed. Land was taken so that the formation could be extended and a 120yds loop line was provided. This made the turn-round of trains easier and later it provided a useful passing place. In this view, No. 2 *The Countess* approaches, piloting visitor *Superior* while a crowded eastbound train passes on the platform road.

82. Welshpool, 1973

Restoration of services to Welshpool was always the aim. Ten years after re-opening, the overgrown line was cleared just sufficiently for *The Earl* to pass with a members' Special on 12 May to be welcomed by the Mayor of Welshpool. A short loop had been provided on the west side of Raven Square when the line was truncated in 1964. A sign of ambition sustained, members supported several trips that weekend. Few thought that in the meadow on the right, a new station would emerge.

83. More Passenger Stock, 1975

A complete train was landed at Liverpool on 7 August 1975, part of the last working on the Sierra Leone Government Railway in West Africa. The four coaches were then delivered, one by one, to Castle Caereinion station for transfer to the W&LLR. At last, the railway had coaches with continuous brakes suitable for use on Golfa bank.

84. SLGR Coach

Gloucester Railway Carriage & Wagon Co Ltd
supplied some 45 coaches to the Sierra Leone
Government Railway in 1961, all with steel bodies
40ft long, mounted on bogies with Timken
bearings. The makers' photograph shows no. 1209
which was fitted out with armchair style seats for
sixteen 1st class passengers. The 3rd class version
had longitudinal wooden slatted seats.
Upholstered seating accommodating up to 50
passengers was installed at Llanfair.
[Gloucester Railway C&W Co Ltd]

85. SLGR Locomotive, 1954

SLGR No. 84 and twin No. 85 were built together
by the Hunslet Engine Co.; the Sierra Leone
Government Railway paid £21,273 for the pair.
They were the last of a line of 32 similar SLGR
engines built for quite long trips. No. 85 was
rescued in 1975 to arrive in Wales with the coaches.
[Hunslet Holdings PLC]

86. The Matary Design

Kerr Stuart & Co of Stoke on Trent specialised in supplying locomotives for colonial estates. The Matary (or Barreto) 0-6-2 design of narrow gauge tank locomotives was first produced in 1912; *Joan*, the twelfth of this type, was built in 1927 with a boiler somewhat larger than standard and a conventional central dome.
[Hunslet Holdings PLC]

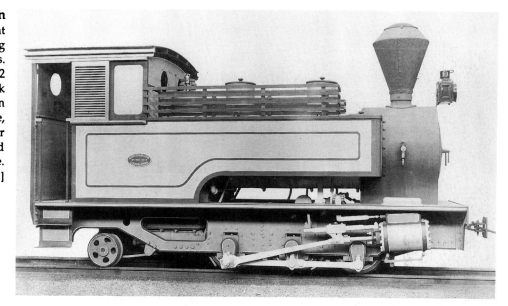

87. *Joan*, 1987

No. 12 *Joan* was spotted abandoned and derelict at a sugar factory on the island of Antigua. Acquisition was far from straight forward but eventually the 0-6-2 tank locomotive was landed at Liverpool on 26 November 1971. Originally an oil burner, it has also used sugar cane waste. Rebuilding in 1949-51 gave it a new Hunslet boiler and full length tanks. After arrival in Wales, a five year major overhaul preceded its entry into service early in 1977. It gained a cab backsheet, vacuum brakes and standard injectors while obtrusive steam feed pumps were removed from the front buffer beam and tank top

88. No. 14 at Castle Caereinion, 1979

Following a major overhaul, former SLGR No. 85 had just entered service on the W&LLR. It has proved an excellent performer and a great favourite with crews. After modifications to the exhaust arrangement in 1993, it proved itself capable of hauling some of the heaviest trains up Golfa bank. It was photographed, Llanfair bound, passing a train for Welshpool.

89. Brynelyn Viaduct, 1976

No. 1 *The Earl* coasts over this substantial six arch structure near Cyfronydd with a train of ex-Upnor and ex-Zillertalbahn stock. The ex-Admiralty coaches did not have continuous brakes and two years later were sold, the four former semi-opens going to the line at Sittingbourne in Kent.

90. No. 6 *Monarch*, 1976
On the switchback section of line between Cyfronydd and Heniarth, this unusual articulated locomotive heads stock
of contrasting designs. A modified Meyer type, *Monarch* arrived on 8 May 1966 from Bowaters Paper Mills in Kent.
When W. G. Bagnall Ltd completed it in 1953, Coronation year, it was the last narrow gauge steam engine
to be built for ordinary commercial service in this country. Eventually, the W&LLR concluded
that the marine firebox and other problems affecting its steaming performance
made it unsuitable for the line andnew owners moved
it to the Festiniog Railway.

91. Extending to Welshpool

In May 1977, the Welshpool Extension Scheme was launched - and an appeal for £63,000. A new station was needed and the 2³/₄ miles of track from Sylfaen to Welshpool, down the steep and twisting Golfa incline, was to be rebuilt. Work soon began on clearing bushes and trees from the trackbed prior to installing new culverts, drains and ballast. With a £20,000 contribution to the fund from the Development Board for Rural Wales and with assistance from a government training scheme, re-laying by volunteers began in mid-section at Golfa siding in August 1979.

92. Preparing Sleepers at Castle Station, 1979

Over 5,000 new sleepers were needed. Imported steel sleepers recovered from the closed Sierra Leone Railway seemed a low cost solution for long life track. Unfortunately, political intrigue and complications in Sierra Leone eventually thwarted the company's efforts and a decision was made to import Australian hardwood sleepers.

93. Welshpool – New Terminus in Embryo, 1979

Land was leased alongside the old line - a swampy meadow with a meandering stream which was diverted into a new channel. The new formation gradually rose by dint of much tipping. The remains of the truncated original line can be seen on the left, heading towards Raven Square road crossing.

94. Raven Square Station, 1981
A month after the extension opened, No. 14 waits beside the temporary platform and a van, derailed, serves as a booking office. With approval from the Department of Transport, public services had started on 18 July with a jubilant ceremony and huge crowds. Resources were stretched and it was not then possible to provide buildings of any sort and a tank on a wagon did duty as a temporary water tower.

95. Raven Square Station, 1992
A recent view shows No.10 *Sîr Drefaldwyn* waiting to attack the 1 in 35 bank out of the station. On 4 July 1981, *Sîr Drefaldwyn* had been the first steam locomotive to enter the new station, hauling a test train. The station gained a substantial platform, signals and a signal box-cum-booking office in time for a ceremony on 16 May 1982 when the 6th Earl of Powis formally inaugurated the now completed extension.

96. Smaller Engines, 1980

The diesel No.11 *Ferret* (left) was one of Hunslet Engine Company's earlier flameproof designs intended for underground work. Completed in 1941 for the Admiralty, it worked in a Wiltshire depot and moved to Llanfair in 1971. Fitted with a 50hp Gardiner 4L2 engine, it proved very successful on engineering trains aided by low gearing. No.8 *Dougal* was also designed to work in limited confines – Glasgow Corporation's Provan Gasworks. Andrew Barclay, Sons & Co supplied it in 1946. Only twelve years later, it was saved from scrapping by enthusiasts and stored. Moved to the W&LLR in 1969, it sees occasional use on demonstration freight trains.

97. Mechanical Engineering, 1979

Dismantled in the workshops at Llanfair, *The Countess* had been out of service since 1970. Its heavy overhaul started in 1978. The boiler was eventually dispatched to contractors for renovation and the locomotive returned to traffic in 1986. Coach B17 was also in the workshops having woodwork replaced.

98. *The Earl* and *The Countess* **Reunited, 1991**

The Earl was withdrawn from service in 1978 needing major repairs. Then, in GWR livery, it was displayed in turn in the National Railway Museum, York, the Birmingham Railway Museum and Didcot Railway Centre. It is seen on the lowloader on its return. After returning to traffic in 1986, No.2 *The Countess* performed reliably and in its Cambrian livery continued to be much admired.
[Margaret Murray]

99. Tanllan Sidings, 1991

Sîr Drefaldwyn passes the outer home signal on the approach to Llanfair station. Stock sidings on the right were laid after reclaiming rough ground in 1975 but another fourteen years elapsed before funds were available for the erection of the 105ft four road carriage shed. On the left of the curve, a siding built for timber loading in 1904 existed for many years and was recently restored for the use of the permanent way department.

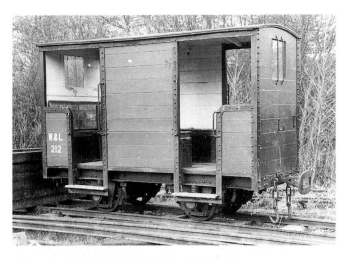

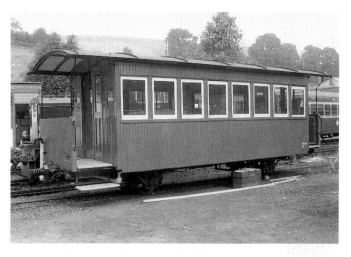

100 & 101. Brake Van/Riding Van 212

A large fleet of vehicles normally used only on permanent way trains has been built up. Originally, this brake van (above) was used on the Lodge Hill & Upnor Railway's ammunition trains. In addition to the original freight stock which was rescued, vehicles have come from a Royal Naval armaments depot in Pembrokeshire, from a Ministry of Defence depot in Cumberland and from Bowaters Paper Mills.

In 1979, the former brake van was rebuilt for the use of maintenance gangs (below). The central brake pillar and its four cast iron weights were removed.

102 & 103. Ziller Coach Rebuilt

After almost 90 years in service, the wooden bodied Zillertalbahn coaches were approaching the end of their life. Fortunately, a training organisation for would-be shipyard apprentices in Birkenhead offered to help. Coach B16 was reconstructed first, followed by B14. The latter is seen (above) on its return from Birkenhead. Double doors were provided at one end of the saloon to allow wheelchair access. Both the Ziller coaches rebuilt were given a steel superstructure clad with woodwork restored to pristine condition. The chassis, running gear and brakegear were also overhauled (below).

104. Raven Square Station, 1993

Pressure for better passenger facilities led to considerable debate about the style of building following rejection of a modernistic design put forward by Powys County Council. When a redundant railway building was offered, it was decided to dismantle it and move it piece by piece to Welshpool. Fully restored (a legacy helped), it was opened with ceremony in 1992. The merit of the prestigious project has attracted several awards.

105. Former Station Building, Eardisley, 1990

This dilapidated potting shed in Herefordshire once served the LMS and GWR having been provided by the Hereford, Hay and Brecon Railway in 1863. The station closed in 1962. Restoration after its move to Welshpool involved new foundations, considerable repairs and chemical treatment to eradicate rot.
[David Taylor]

106. Golfa, 1981

No. 14 (ex-SLR No.85) pauses at Golfa siding. Almost immediately after leaving Welshpool, the train has climbed the 1 in 29 mile-long incline with its notorious reverse curves. Some crews stand at Golfa to raise steam before tackling the remaining 1 in 41 climb to the summit. All crossings are simple: most are open (though with cattle grids).

107. Upgrading the Permanent Way, 1993

In the years following re-opening, most of the line between Llanfair and Sylfaen was relaid with redundant ex-BR softwood sleeper halves. Better sleepers were later found and in 1993, a large quantity of very substantial mostly new ex-NATO concrete sleepers was acquired. Such material (and such quality) is rare on the narrow gauge in Britain. New techniques of handling had to be developed.

[Eileen Niblock]

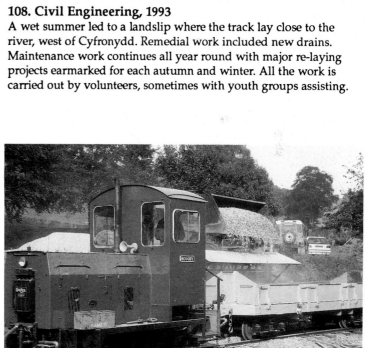

108. Civil Engineering, 1993

A wet summer led to a landslip where the track lay close to the river, west of Cyfronydd. Remedial work included new drains. Maintenance work continues all year round with major re-laying projects earmarked for each autumn and winter. All the work is carried out by volunteers, sometimes with youth groups assisting.

109. No.16 *Scooby*, 1994

A ballast train being loaded at Tanllan siding, Llanfair, is headed by the 0-4-0 Hunslet *Scooby* which recently entered service on the line. It was rebuilt at Llanfair from the original mines-type design, identical to No. 11 *Ferret* (see photograph no. 94). This World War II 50hp diesel arrived in 1992 from a NATO depot in Cumberland.

110. Arriving at Llanfair Station, 1980

As No. 12 *Joan* approaches with a train from Welshpool, the signalman receives the train staff. A divisible staff allows trains to follow in the same direction but locomotive crews must be in possession of the appropriate instrument for authority to move along the single line. It is divided into block sections at Cyfronydd, Castle Caereinion and Sylfaen. There is also radio communication between trains and signal box, introduced in 1994.

111. Cancelled

"Floods – no trains today." A disappointment for this family at Llanfair station. It is only rarely that services are suspended; the proximity of the River Banwy near the western end of the line makes it vulnerable to flooding at times of unusually heavy rainfall.

112. Llanfair Station: the Long Shed, 1993

Erected for the opening in 1903 and extended in 1915, the goods shed was taken over by preservationists in 1962. It then provided valuable accommodation for the engineering department despite its dilapidated appearance.

113. Llanfair Station Building, 1994

The decision to provide new passenger facilities called for a design to reflect the line's heritage. The old 'Long Shed' was restored, converted and extended to provide a period tea room, booking office and souvenir shop. A substantial grant from the European Regional Development Fund swelled the Appeal Fund.

114. Taking Water, 1989

Special events became a feature of the programme to boost traffic. The 'Friends of Thomas the Tank Engine' weekends are popular with children and on these occasions *Joan* has become a particular favourite: the change of livery from maroon to blue was timely. The locomotive was running with a chimney borrowed from No. 14.

115. *Chevallier*, 1991

The annual 'Steam Galas' attract crowds of enthusiasts. A guest locomotive often provides a special treat. 0–6–2T *Chevallier*, built by Manning Wardle in 1915 for the Lodge Hill & Upnor Railway came from Whipsnade Zoo and is seen assisting *The Countess* on the approach to Sylfaen.

116. *Superior*, 1992
Another visitor arrived from Whipsnade's Zoo railway the following autumn. This 0–6–2 Kerr Stuart belonged, like *Joan*, to the maker's Matary class but was a standard version (see photograph no. 82). Delivered in 1920, it worked at Bowaters Paper Mills in Kent.

117. Hoboken Steelworks No. 6, 1993
This guest locomotive came from another Kent line. The Bredgar & Wormshill Light Railway had just restored this attractive little machine after rescuing it from a contractor's yard in Belgium. The steelworks where it spent its working life was near Antwerp. Built by La Meuse at Liege in 1929, the locomotive is seen at Llanfair at the end of its first run in this country.

118. *Siam*, 1994

The W&LLR's Steam Gala event provided the opportunity for this 0-6-0 side/well tank to make its debut in service. Visiting from the Bredgar & Wormshill Light Railway, its gauge prevents it from running on the line there. Built in Henschel's works in Germany in 1956, it was shipped to the Chamburi Sugar Factory in Thailand and worked as their No. 105 until about 1969. In the 1980s it arrived in Britain, finally moving to Bredgar to be superbly restored. [K. I. Bond]

119. Mixed Train, 1988

The Countess heads eastwards near Dolrhyd Mill on 10 September 1988 hauling stock which includes an ex-Bowaters Paper Mill open wagon, a GWR-built cattle van and an original 1902 brake van. Unfortunately, the two original brake vans were destroyed by fire but the building of a replica started in 1990. Mixed trains are provided from time to time on charter for enthusiasts' groups.

Gala Weekend 1994

WORKING TIMETABLE & STAFF ROSTER
3rd & 4th September 1994

BLOCKPOSTS OPEN: Llanfair (Control)   Cyfronydd
Castle   Sylfaen
Welshpool

Train No.		P1	P3	P5	P7	W91	P9	P11	P13	P15
LLANFAIR	dep.	08.30t	09.30	10.45	12.00t	12.20	13.30	14.45	16.15	18.30
Heniarth	dep.	08r39t	09r39	10r54	12r09t	12.30	13r39	14r54	16r24	18r39
Cyfronydd	dep.	08r54t	09r45	11r00	12r14t	12a40	13r45	15r00	16r30	18r45
Castle	dep.	08.57t	09.55	11.12	12.27		13.57	15.12	16.42	18.57
SYLFAEN	arr.	09.02t	10X00	11X16	12X31		14X01	15X16	16X46	
	dep.	09.03	10X01	11X17	12X32		14X02	15X17	16X47	19r03
WELSHPOOL	arr.	09.20	10.20	11.35	12.50		14.20	15.35	17.05	19.20

Train No.		P2	P4	P6	W92	P8	P10	P12	P14	P16
WELSHPOOL	dep.	09.45	11.00b	12.15b		13.45b	15.00b	16.30	17.15	19.40
SYLFAEN	arr.	09X58	11X14	12X29		13X59	15X14	16X44	17.29	
	dep.	10X02	11X18	12X33		14X03	15X18	16X48t	17.30	19r53
Castle		10.07	11.22	12.37		14.07	15.22	16.52t	17.37	20.02
Cyfronydd	dep.	10r18	11r33	12.48t	13.05	14r18	15r33	17r03t	17r48	20r13
Heniarth	dep.	10r26	11r41	12.56t	13.15	14r26	15r41	17r11t	17r56	20r21
LLANFAIR	arr.	10.35	11.50	13.05t	13.25	14.35	15.50	17.20t	18.05	20.30

NOTES:

a = arrival time
b = In the event of this train being fully booked, it may depart up to 5 minutes early.
r = train stops on request
t = Driver to be issued with TICKET for single line section, having
    been shown the STAFF COMPLETE WITH BOTH TICKETS first.
X = trains cross
W91&W92 = Freight trains

SYLFAEN WILL BE A COMPULSORY STOP ON TRIPS WHEN TRAINS ARE BOOKED TO CROSS
Trains travelling towards Llanfair which are halted at the STOP board at Castle Blockpost
    will be called into the Station by radio. Guards will give a "proceed" signal to the
    Driver upon receipt of the radio message.

120. Working Timetable, 1994

121. Boiler Work, 1994

In 1994, soon after a major overhaul of No. 15 *Orion* had begun, the boiler was lifted and prepared for a full inspection. This indicated that extensive (and expensive) repair work would be needed including a new firebox.

122. No. 15 *Orion* in 1984: Latent Power

The original home of this massive 2-6-2 tank (weighing 33 tons) was on the Jokioisten Railway in southern Finland. It was supplied in 1948 by Tubize of Belgium and ran until 1969. Saved from the scrap merchant by an English enthusiast, it languished in store until it was acquired by the W&LLR in 1983. Of a relatively modern design, this should prove an easy locomotive to maintain with adequate power for hauling heavy trains up the W&LLR's dramatically steep grades.

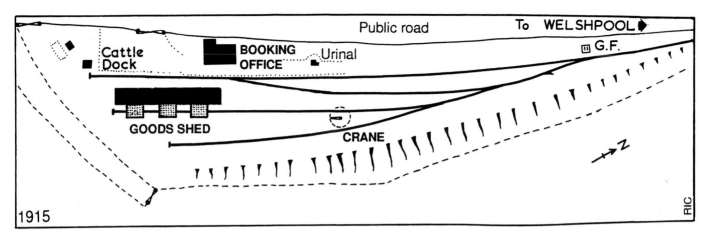

123. Llanfair Station, 1915.

124. Llanfair Station, 1995

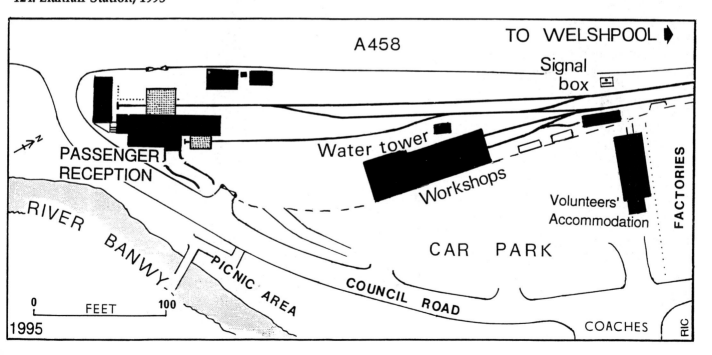

W&L no.	Name	Type	Builder's details	Date of arrival	Notes
1	*The Earl*	0-6-0T	Beyer Peacock, 1902	1902	Rebuilt GWR 1929 to BR Oswestry 1958 returned 1961
2	*The Countess*	0-6-0T	Beyer Peacock, 1902	1902	Rebuilt GWR 1930 to BR Oswestry 1956 returned 1962
3	*Raven*	4wD	Ruston & Hornsby, 1934	1961	Sold 1974
4	*Upnor Castle*	4wD	Hibbert (Planet), 1954	1962	Sold 1968
5	*Nutty*	0-4-0VB	Sentinel, 1929	1964	Transferred 1971
6	*Monarch*	0-4-4-0T	Bagnall, 1953	1966	Sold 1992
7	*Chattenden*	0-6-0D	Baguley (Drewry), 1949	1968	
8	*Dougal*	0-4-0T	Barclay, 1946	1969	
9	*Wynnstay*	0-6-0D	Fowler, 1951	1969	Sold 1972
10	*Sîr Drefaldwyn*	0-8-0T	Franco-Belge, 1944	1969	
11	*Ferret*	0-4-0D	Hunslet, 1940-1	1971	
12	*Joan*	0-6-2T	Kerr Stuart, 1927	1971	
14	*SLR No. 85*	2-6-2T	Hunslet 1954	1975	
15	*Orion*	2-6-2T	Tubize, 1948	1983	
16	*Scooby*	0-4-0D	Hunslet, 1941-2	1992	Rebuilt 1993

125. Stock List: Locomotives

No.	Type (seating capacity)	Builder's Details	Date of arrival	Notes
1, 2	1st/brake/3rd (36)	Pickering, 1902	1902	GWR 6338 & 6466 scrapped 1936
3	All 3rd (46)	Pickering, 1902	1902	GWR 4154 scrapped 1936
196, 199, 200, 204	Semi-open toastrack (converted to closed) (40)	Cravens, 1941	1961 [1]	Sold 1978
214	'Combination' (2 saloons/brake)	Wickham, 1957	1961 [1]	Sold 1989
B14	End balconies, wooden body* (32)	Grazer, 1900	1968 [2]	
B16	End balconies, wooden body* (32)	Grazer, 1901	1968 [2]	
B17	End balconies, wooden body (32)	Grazer, 1901	1968 [2]	
B24	End balconies, steel body (28)	Grazer, 1925	1968 [2]	
B27	End balconies, steel body (32)	Grazer, 1906	1968 [2]	
1040	Originally 3rd; now stores vehicle	Gloucester C&W, 1961	1975 [3]	
1066, 1048	Originally 3rd; now with 50 seats & brake compartment	Gloucester C&W, 1961	1975 [3]	
1207	Originally 1st; now with 50 seats & brake compartment	Gloucester C&W, 1961	1975 [3]	

Notes
(1) from Lodge Hill & Upnor Railway
(2) from Zillertalbahn, Austria
(3) from Sierra Leone Railway
* B14 & B16 rebuilt with steel body underframing; seating capacity 30.
All vehicles are bogie stock except B14-B27.

126. Stock List: Coaches

Modern Times

On a glorious June evening in 1988, specialist caterers served a fine meal on board a train of vintage Zillertalbahn saloons waiting at scenic Castle Caereinion station. The 'Champagne Dining Train' (the railway's first ever) was one way of celebrating the 25th anniversary of re-opening.

Another first, the previous December, had been Santa specials between Llanfair and Cyfronydd with decorated coaches (and stations), seasonal music and refreshments and the jovial character himself dispensing presents on the trains. Special events of other kinds during the summer season, some for children and some for enthusiasts, have added interest and boosted traffic figures. Unusual events have included the visit of two flywheel-propelled electric-powered tram vehicles in 1994!

Striving to overcome vicissitudes is the essence of life on a preserved line. Although a plan to extend services to Welshpool was mooted in 1966, a decade was to pass before a scheme was adopted. The increasing urgency of rebuilding the western end of the line, the requirement to provide vacuum braked stock, the search for suitable permanent way materials and, of course, the need to find adequate funds all held up restoration of Welshpool services. Raven Square station opened in 1981 with the work having cost almost £75,000, part of which was provided by grants from public funds. Overhauls and mechanical breakdowns were all the more difficult to cope with until the workshops and machine shop could be erected at Llanfair station. Renovation of the freight vehicles has had to take a low priority but rebuilding of the original stock is gradually taking place. Another challenge was that of finding suitable coal for the locomotives as a result of changes in the coal industry. However, recent innovations have included modifications to smokebox components which have improved the performance of the locomotives by up to 20%. The civil engineering department remainsready to carry out work to safeguard the Banwy river bridge, happily saved in 1965.

Recent years have brought steadily rising membership with a welcome boost in 1991 when the Vale of Rheidol Railway Supporters Association dissolved, merging its members and funds with the W&LLR following the sale of the Rheidol line into private ownership. Meanwhile, the railway was fortunate to survive the country's economic recession without traffic suffering.

Most recently, both Welshpool and Llanfair Caereinion stations have been turned into terminals with considerable charm. Nor did the rebuilding schemes overlook the needs of the volunteers who have been instrumental in making the line so successful. A new building, the traditional design of which quickly attracted a local authority award, was erected close to Llanfair station, to provide facilities for them. With the cost of these schemes amounting to around £370,000, grant aid from the European Union was critical to augment funds generously bequeathed and donated.

The development of a host of new ideas has promoted widened interest and ensured that the railway is now established as one of the best-known tourist attractions of mid-Wales, conscious of its role as custodian of part of the national (and international) heritage collection.

In the decades since the W&LLR re-opened, the endeavours of many dedicated volunteers have achieved a remarkable transformation. Visitors travel from far and wide for the experience of storming Golfa incline in one of the turn of the century Austrian balcony coaches behind the railway's sturdy little tank locomotives, perhaps riding back along the Banwy valley in the agreeably comfortable West African bogie saloons.

Efforts to upgrade track, locomotives and stations will stand the railway in good stead as it heads for its centenary. Trains en route now communicate with signalling staff by radio. More developments to look forward to include the entry into service of the massive Tubize locomotive, and later of No. 1 *The Earl*, after a major overhaul. Who knows, perhaps a scheme may also emerge for the building of a replica of the original coaches.